# Turning Your Hobby into a 6-Figure Business

A Step-by-Step Guide

**Dr. Miles J. Cooper**

# Disclaimer

The information in Turning Your Hobby into a 6-Figure Business: A Step-by-Step Guide is for educational and informational purposes only. While every effort has been made to ensure the accuracy and reliability of the content, this book is not a substitute for professional financial, legal, or business advice. Readers are encouraged to consult qualified professionals for personalized guidance tailored to their circumstances.

The strategies, methods, and examples presented are based on general principles and may not guarantee success. Business outcomes can vary depending on market conditions, individual effort, and unforeseen challenges. The author and publisher disclaim any liability for actions taken based on the content of this book.

By using the information in this book, you acknowledge and accept that building a business involves risks, and success is not guaranteed. Your journey is your responsibility, and this book serves as a tool to help you along the way.

All rights reserved. No part of this publication may be reproduced, distributed, or transmitted in any form or by any means, including photocopying, recording, or another electronic or mechanical method without the prior written permission of the publisher except in the case of brief citation embodied in critical reviews and certain other noncommercial use permitted by copyright law.

Copyright @Dr. Miles J. Cooper

Turning Your Hobby into a 6-Figure

# Table of contents

Introduction

### Part 1: Laying the Foundation for Success

Chapter 1: Identifying a Profitable Hobby

Chapter 2: Shaping Your Business Vision

Chapter 3: Understanding the Basics of Business Setup

### Part 2: Building a Strong Business Framework

Chapter 4: Creating Your Brand Identity

Chapter 5: Pricing Strategies that Work

Chapter 6: Designing a Winning Business Plan

### Part 3: Attracting and Growing Your Customer Base

Chapter 7: Marketing Your Hobby Business Effectively

Chapter 8: Selling Strategies for Success

Chapter 9: The Power Of Networking And Collaboration

### Part 4: Scaling and Sustaining Growth

Chapter 10: Automating and Streamlining Operations

Chapter 11: Diversifying Your Income Streams

Chapter 12: Overcoming Challenges in Scaling

### Part 5: Thriving as a 6-Figure Business Owner

Chapter 13: Mastering Your Entrepreneurial Mindset

Conclusion

# Introduction

**The Hobby-to-Business Transformation**

The journey from chasing after a hobby to maintaining a flourishing six-figure business is both enabling and unique. This begins as an individual passion — maybe something you do to relax or put yourself out there — can develop into revenue, satisfaction, and reason. It's not just about transforming a diversion into a benefit; it's tied in with utilizing your remarkable abilities and interests to make a business that reflects your identity.

This change is feasible for anybody who can leap. Whether you're a talented craftsman, a well-informed gamer, an energetic cook, or somebody with an eye for planning, your hobby could become more than a sideline activity. The key lies in understanding how to change from doing the thing you love for the sake of entertainment to building a practical business that aligns with your objectives and values.

The process could appear overwhelming, particularly if maintaining a business feels unfamiliar or overpowering. In any case, with the right direction, clear strategies, and the certainty to embrace the obscure, you can transform your passion into a strong revenue source. This guide is intended to walk you through each step of the journey, offering common sense counsel, note-value experiences, and motivation to assist you with succeeding.

**Why Your Passion Can Be Productive**

Passion is a strong driver of progress. At the point when you emotionally put resources into something, it shows like your work, the excitement you bring to your endeavors, and your capacity to associate with other people who share your preferences. To this end, organizations based on passion frequently outflank those determined simply by benefit.

Be that as it may, how might a hobby convert into a productive business? It starts with perceiving that your one-of-a-kind ability, information, and imagination have value in the commercial focus. Individuals will pay for top-notch items, services, or encounters that take special care of their requirements and wants. Whether it's hand-tailored adornments, custom photography, wellness instructing, or advanced items, your passion can tackle issues, satisfy wants, or proposition bliss to your target audience.

Productivity isn't just about bringing in cash; it's tied in with building a plan of action that upholds development, supportability, and long-term success. This includes understanding your audience, making an exceptional selling recommendation (USP), and decisively situating your contributions in a way that resounds with possible customers.

At the point when you're driven by passion, you're bound to conquer difficulties, remain spurred, and convey outstanding value to your customers. This emotional venture can separate your business and prepare you for financial success.

**Defeating Doubts and Mindset Shifts for Progress**
Perhaps the greatest impediment in transforming a hobby into a business is self-question. Many hopeful business visionaries wonder whether or not to dive in, addressing whether their abilities are sufficient, their thoughts are adequately novel, or whether they're ready to deal with the pioneering scene. These questions are typical, but they shouldn't keep you down.

Success starts with a mindset shift. Rather than review your hobby as "for no reason in particular," begin seeing it as an establishment for something more prominent. This doesn't mean you want to surrender the delight it brings — all things being equal, it's tied in with figuring out how to adjust passion and benefit. Taking on a development outlook is fundamental, as it assists you with embracing difficulties, gaining from disappointments, and remaining focused on your objectives.

One more basic outlook shift includes considering yourself to be an entrepreneur. This could require venturing outside your usual range of familiarity, mastering new abilities, and settling on choices that vibe new. Nonetheless, every step you take will bring you nearer to the certainty and skill expected to build a fruitful business.

Keep in mind, that no fruitful business person begins with every one of the responses. The key is to remain open to learning, look for help when required, and trust in your capacity to adjust and develop. By tending to your questions head-on and reexamining your viewpoint, you can get yourself positioned for long-term success.

This book will act as your manual for exploring the hobby-to-business venture. Every section is intended to give note value systems, master bits of knowledge, and motivation to assist you with conquering hindrances and accomplishing your objectives. Whether you're simply beginning or hoping to scale your current business, this bit-by-bit guide will enable you to transform your passion into a flourishing six-figure adventure.

Your process starts here. How about we open your true capacity and construct the matter of your fantasies?

# Part 1: Laying the Foundation for Success

# CHAPTER 1: IDENTIFYING A PROFITABLE HOBBY

**Assessing Your Hobby's Potential**

The first step to transforming your hobby into a six-figure business is distinguishing whether it can be productive. While passion is fundamental, assessing the attractiveness of your hobby is similarly significant. A fruitful hobby finds some harmony between what you love doing and what others will pay for.

Begin by considering the value your hobby brings to other people. Does it solve a particular issue, satisfy a need, or bring happiness and fulfillment? For instance, baking could offer solace and festivity, while making custom jewelry permits people to express their exceptional style. The more value your hobby gives, the more prominent its true capacity as a business.

Then, check out your abilities and aptitude. Are you capable in your specialty as of now, or do you need to invest in additional learning? While you needn't bother with being an expert to begin, having a strong foundation can assist you with delivering great contributions that entice customers.

Surveying your commitment is additionally fundamental. Transforming a hobby into a business calls for investment, effort, and in some cases penance. Consider whether you're willing to devote yourself to scaling and supporting your hobby as an undertaking.

**Understanding Market Demand**

A productive hobby isn't just about your passion — it's tied to fulfilling market needs. Exploring the market assists you with deciding if there's an audience of people for your items or services. Begin by investigating who could profit from or appreciate what you offer. Who are your possible customers? What are their preferences, trouble spots, and buying habits?

One powerful method for measuring demand is through online research. Platforms like Google Patterns, Etsy, Pinterest, and Amazon can give bits of knowledge into what individuals are looking for and purchasing. For instance, assuming you make hand-tailored candles, check whether they're moving into home style and gift classes. Social media platforms can likewise uncover patterns and customer intrigues in your specialty.

Also, investigate your opposition. Recognize other people who are adapting comparative leisure activities and study their contributions, evaluating systems, and customer commitment. This examination can assist you with understanding what works, what holes exist on the lookout, and how you can separate your business.

Try things out by offering your item or service on a limited scale. Whether it's setting up a corner at a local market or posting things online, early feedback can assist you with fine-tuning your contributions and affirming your demand.

## Finding Your Unique Selling Proposition (USP)

In a competitive commercial focus, having serious areas of unique selling proposition (USP) is fundamental. Your USP separates your hobby business from others. It's the explanation customers pick you over contenders, and it imparts the particular value you offer that would be useful.

1. To recognize your USP, think about these inquiries:
2. What makes your items or services unique or better?
3. How would you address your customer's requirements in a manner others don't?
4. What individual contacts or aptitude do you bring to your work?

For instance, assuming you're a photographic artist, your USP may be working in open minutes that recount a story. In the event that you're a pastry specialist, it very well may be utilizing natural, privately obtained elements for well-being, cognizant customers.

Featuring your USP draws in customers as well as builds your brand personality. It conveys your main goal, values, and what your business depends on. Integrate your USP into your advertising endeavors, item descriptions, and customer connections to reliably support what makes you exceptional.

Distinguishing a beneficial hobby is the foundation of your business process. By assessing your hobby's true capacity, understanding business sector interest, and defining your special selling suggestion, you lay the basis for a business that is fruitful as well as emotionally fulfilling. As you push ahead, recall that benefit begins with passion but blossoms with the procedure. With cautious preparation and an unmistakable vision, you're one bit nearer to building a flourishing six-figure business.

# CHAPTER 2: SHAPING YOUR BUSINESS VISION

A convincing business vision is the foundation of any effective entrepreneurial journey. It gives guidance, energizes inspiration, and fills in as a directing light when difficulties emerge. Molding your business vision starts with clearness about your objectives, a rousing mission and vision explanation, and an individual meaning of progress. Together, these components make a structure that keeps your business on target and lined up with your interests and values.

**Putting forth Clear Objectives**

Objectives change dreams into significant steps. To build a flourishing 6-figure business, you want objectives that are specific, quantifiable, reachable, important, and time-bound. Begin by recognizing momentary targets that set the establishment, like launching an item, making a site, or getting your most memorable deal.

Similarly, significant are long-term objectives that mirror your goals for the future, like scaling your business, accomplishing financial freedom, or making an inheritance. Break these bigger objectives into more modest success, making the way to progress more sensible. Recording your objectives on paper and returning to them consistently keeps you engaged and responsible.

Keep in mind, that your objectives ought to line up with your qualities and vision. Try not to seek after objectives that don't resonate with your interests or lead to burnout. All things considered, focus on objectives that rouse you and add to a feasible business.

**Making a Mission and Vision Statement**

A statement of purpose explains your motivation, while a dream statement frames your desires. Together, they define why your business exists and what you desire to accomplish. These assertions furnish clearness as well as resound with customers who share your qualities.

Your statement of purpose ought to respond to key inquiries:
1. How does your business respond?
2. Who does it serve?

3. How can it create value?

For instance, a jewelry producer's central goal could be: "To create immortal, eco-accommodating jewelry that enables people and celebrates maintainability."

Your vision statement, then again, ought to portray the future you need to make. It's optimistic and forward-looking. Going on with the jewelry model, a dream may be: "To turn into a universally perceived pioneer reasonably, motivating a development toward moral commercialization."

Keep these statements concise, legal, and lined up with your interests. They are words on a page as well as a wellspring of motivation that directs your choices and interfaces you with your audience.

## Defining Success Based on Your Terms

Success appears to be unique for everybody, and it's pivotal to define how it affects you. While financial success is much of the time underscored, genuine progress incorporates more than income. Think about these aspects:

1. Individual Satisfaction: Does your business line up with your interests and give you pleasure?
2. Influence: Would you say you are having an effect in the existence of your customers or local area?
3. Work-Life Balance: Would you say you are ready to keep up with the concordance between your business and individual life?

Defining accomplishment based on your conditions assists you with keeping fixed on the main thing, staying away from the traps of correlation or cultural strain. Your vision of success could incorporate financial autonomy, artistic liberty, or the capacity to help causes you care about.

As you develop, return to your meaning of progress and change it depending on the situation. Your needs might advance, and your business ought to adjust likewise.

Turning Your Hobby into a 6-Figure

Molding your business vision is definitely not a one-time movement; it's a continuous interaction. Return to your objectives, mission, and vision routinely to guarantee they stay significant and moving. As you accomplish success, praise your advancement and refine your way ahead.

With a reasonable vision, you're not simply maintaining a business — you're building an inheritance that mirrors your qualities, interests, and goals. By remaining consistent with your vision, you'll explore difficulties with certainty and make a business that is both satisfying and effective.

# CHAPTER 3: UNDERSTANDING THE BASICS OF BUSINESS SETUP

**Choosing a Business Structure**

Transforming your hobby into a real business begins with picking the right business structure. This choice affects your legal and burden commitments as well as shapes how you work and develop your business.

For most specialists progressing to a business venture, beginning as a sole proprietorship or a solitary part LLC is normal. Sole proprietorship is the least complex structure and permits you to work under your name or an enrolled business name. Be that as it may, it doesn't give responsibility security, meaning your resources could be in danger assuming that the business causes obligations or lawful issues.

On the other hand, forming a limited liability company (LLC) offers individual responsibility security while keeping up with functional adaptability. This is an appealing choice for some entrepreneurs since it separates your own business funds.

Different designs, like corporations or partnerships, may suit bigger endeavors with numerous proprietors or high-development potential. No matter what your decision is, counseling a lawful or financial consultant can assist you with deciding the best fit for your particular necessities.

Whenever you've settled on a structure, guarantee you understand the lawful and charge suggestions. Enrolling your business with the fitting neighborhood, state, or government specialists is basic to working lawfully and keeping away from fines.

**Registering Your Business and Taking Care of Legalities**

Legal compliance is a vital stage in legitimizing your business. Begin by choosing a business name that mirrors your brand and resounds with your target audience. Actually take a look at the accessibility of the name through your state's business library and guarantee it's not currently reserved.

Then, register your business with the fitting government specialists. This might incorporate acquiring an employer identification Number (EIN) from the IRS, which is vital for charge purposes, regardless of whether you intend to recruit workers. Contingent upon your industry and area, you could likewise require specific allowances or licenses to lawfully work.

For instance, on the off chance that you're selling prepared products, you might require food dealing with grants. Assuming your hobby includes offering services like wellness training, you could require certificates or risk protection. Exploring your industry's legal necessities guarantees you're completely ready to work without pointless interference.

Moreover, starting a committed business bank account separates your own business funds, improving accounting and expense planning. Many banks offer particular records for private companies, frequently with advantages like lower expenses or accommodating instruments for business people.

## Fundamental Tools and Resources to Get Everything Started

Beginning your business requires more than passion — it takes the right instruments and resources to build areas of strength for a. Luckily, numerous reasonable or even free tools can assist you with smoothing out activities, dealing with your time, and associating with your audience.

For financial service, tools like QuickBooks, Wave, or FreshBooks assist you with tracking pay, costs, and taxes. These platforms additionally make invoicing and planning clear, so you can focus in on developing your business as opposed to doing the math.

With regards to internet business platforms, Shopify, Etsy, and Squarespace permit you to make an expert online-based store to showcase your items or services. These platforms are beginner-friendly and incorporate highlights like installment handling, stock service, and promoting instruments.

Social media management tools like Hootsuite can save time by booking and automating posts across numerous platforms. Consistent social media commitment is fundamental for marketing, and these instruments assist you with remaining coordinated without feeling overpowered.

Assuming that your hobby includes making advanced items or instructive substance, platforms like Canva (for design) or Workable (for online courses) give proficient outcomes without requiring broad specialized abilities.

Remember the force of networking and mentorship. Local business improvement focuses, online networks, and connections like SCORE offer free or minimal-expense workshop, mentorship projects, and resources custom-fitted to entrepreneurs. These connections can give important direction as you explore the difficulties of business ventures.

Understanding the essentials of business arrangement changes your hobby into a tenable and manageable endeavor. By picking the right design, meeting legal prerequisites, and utilizing fundamental tools, you make a strong starting point for development. While the setup process might appear to be intricate, each step carries you closer to accomplishing your innovative dreams. With cautious preparation and the right resources, your hobby can develop into a flourishing business that upholds your financial and individual objectives.

# Part 2: Building a Strong Business Framework

# CHAPTER 4: CREATING YOUR BRAND IDENTITY

**Developing a Memorable Brand Name and Logo**

Your brand identity starts with a name and logo that epitomizes the quintessence of your business. A strong brand name is something beyond a mark — it's the first feeling customers have of your business and ought to convey your qualities, reason, and character.

While conceptualizing a name, consider how it mirrors your hobby, lines up with your target audience, and reverberates inside your specialty. Hold back nothing, simple to articulate, and critical. For instance, if your hobby includes high-quality earthenware, a name like "Earthly Creations" recommends credibility and craftsmanship while associating with natural materials.

After choosing a name, design a logo that outwardly addresses your brand. A logo is a strong brand that cultivates acknowledgment and trust. Keep it straightforward but significant — clean lines, adjusted colors, and a reasonable plan are many times more compelling than excessively complex illustrations.

In the event that design isn't your strength, use tools like Canva or employ an independent graphic designer through platforms, for example, Fiverr or Upwork. Be purposeful about your variety design and typography; colors inspire feelings, and textual styles mirror your brand's tone. For example, strong textual styles and splendid varieties can project passion and excitement, while pastel tones and prearranged textual styles recommend class and tranquility.

Keep in mind, that consistency across your name, logo, and other branding components is fundamental for laying out a firm and expert brand.

## Laying out Your Brand Story and Guiding principle

A convincing brand story is a scaffold among you and your audience. It refines your business, builds emotional connections, and recognizes you from contenders. Start by pondering why you began your hobby and how it developed into a business. Feature your passion, battles, and forward leaps to make a story that customers see as engaging and motivating.

For instance, assuming your hobby includes baking and your process started with reproducing family recipes, share the story behind those recipes and how they motivated your business. Authenticity is vital — individuals are attracted to certified stories that reverberate with their own encounters.

Close to your story, articulate your fundamental beliefs. These are the core values that shape your business choices and connections with customers. Instances of guiding principle could incorporate maintainability, imagination, inclusivity, or quality craftsmanship. Ensure your activities and branding reliably mirror these qualities to construct believability and trust.

Your brand story and values ought to be woven into your site, social media profiles, and marketing materials. Doing so builds up your brand identity and encourages faithfulness among your audience.

## Situating Your Brand in a Competitive Market

Situating your brand successfully includes cutting out an unmistakable spot in your industry and laying out your exceptional value to customers. Begin by directing an exhaustive investigation of your rivals. Distinguish what they get along admirably, where they miss the mark, and how you can separate your brand.

Focus around your unique selling proposition (USP) — the particular quality that separates your business. This could be anything from creative designs to predominant customer service or eco-accommodating materials. For example, assuming your hobby includes making jewelry, your USP may be offering customized designs created from practical materials.

Turning Your Hobby into a 6-Figure

Understand your main target audience's needs, preferences, and problem areas, then tailor your information to straightforwardly address them. Impart the advantages your items or services give and how they work in your customers' lives.

Leverage your branding to lay out an emotional connection with your audience. Individuals don't simply purchase items; they purchase the experiences and feelings related to them. Make a character that reverberates emotionally with your customers, whether it's through optimistic informing, humor, or a feeling of the local area.

However, guarantee your branding is reliable across all channels, including your site, social media, and bundling. Consistency builds up trust and makes your brand effectively conspicuous in a packed commercial focus.

By focusing in on a memorable name, a real story, and a vital market situation, you lay the preparation for a brand character that sticks out. Your brand is more than a logo or slogan — it's the essence of your business and the connection you build with your customers. A strong, distinct brand character draws in customers as well as moves devotion, transforming one-time purchasers into long-lasting allies.

# CHAPTER 5: PRICING STRATEGIES THAT WORK

**Calculating Costs and Setting Profit Margins**

Pricing is one of the most basic parts of your business system. It influences your benefit as well as impacts how customers see your brand. To set a value that works, you should firstly compute your expenses precisely.

Start by separating your costs into two classes: fixed expenses and variable expenses. Fixed costs incorporate costs like equipment, lease (if appropriate), and software subscription — costs that stay steady paying little heed to creation. Variable expenses, then again, incorporate materials, bundling, and delivery — costs that vary in light of the volume of items or services you give.

Whenever you've determined your absolute expenses, decide your ideal net revenue. A net revenue addresses the level of income that surpasses your expenses. For instance, if your complete expense to produce an item is $20 and you need a half overall revenue, your cost would be $30.

To remain competitive, research the market and investigate the evaluating of comparable items or services. Be careful not to underestimate your contributions by setting prices excessively low, as this can prompt dainty edges and customer view of bad quality. Then again, unreasonably exorbitant prices could estrange your main target audience. Take a stab at an equilibrium that mirrors the value of your item while taking care of your expenses and guaranteeing benefit.

**Understanding Value-Based Pricing**

Value based pricing goes past taking care of expenses and means to value your item or service in light of the value it gives to your customers. This strategy expects you to understand your customers emotionally — what they value, what issues they face, and how your contribution tackles those issues.

For example, assuming that your hobby includes making custom work of art, customers are not only paying for the material or paint; they're putting resources into a unique, customized piece that holds wistful value. In such cases, the cost ought to mirror the emotional and tasteful value of the item, in addition to the materials and work included.

Situating your item as a top notch offering can legitimize greater prices, giving you unique quality and an exceptional customer experience. For instance, handcrafted items or customized benefits frequently order more exorbitant prices since they are seen as restrictive and stand-out.

It is pivotal to communicate this value. Utilize your branding, storytelling, and advertising materials to emphasize the advantages and interesting parts of your item. Show customers why your contribution merits the venture, whether it's through tributes, nitty gritty item portrayals, or outwardly engaging introductions.

**Offering Discount and Packages without Subverting Value**

Discount and special packages can be powerful instruments to draw in customers, support sales, and clear stock. Notwithstanding, these strategies should be utilized mindfully to abstain from debasing your item or disintegrating your net revenues.

Begin by defining clear goals for your discounts. Might it be said that you are presenting another item, uplifting rehash business, or drawing in first-time customers? For example, offering a little discount on a customer's most memorable buy can boost them to attempt your item while building generosity.

Packages or bundles are another successful procedure. Assuming your hobby includes skincare items, you could make a "starter pack" that incorporates a chemical, toner, and cream at a somewhat scaled down value contrasted with purchasing everything separately. This empowers bigger buys as well as acquaints customers with a scope of your items.

Be aware of how much of the time you offer discounts. Constant sales can condition customers to wait for price drops, lessening the apparent value of your item. All things being equal, use discounts sparingly and decisively, for example, during occasions or unique occasions.

Furthermore, guarantee your discounts lineup with your general evaluating strategy. A 10% discount on a high-edge item might in any case leave you with a strong benefit, while a similar rebate on a low-edge thing could bring about a misfortune. Continuously assess the financial effect of your advancements prior to carrying out them.

By dominating pricing techniques, you not just guarantee the financial soundness of your business but in addition make a view of significant value that resounds with your customers. Pricing is something beyond numbers — it's an amazing asset for situating your brand, imparting quality, and cultivating trust. At the point when done well, it prepares for sustainable development and long-term success.

# CHAPTER 6: DESIGNING A WINNING BUSINESS PLAN

**Breaking Down a Simple Business Plan Template**

A very organized strategy is a guide for your hobby-to-business venture. It gives clarity, direction, and a system to gauge progress. While traditional marketable strategies can be extensive and complex, you can make a smoothed-out variant customized to your requirements, focusing in on the fundamentals that will direct your development.

Begin with the executive summary, a succinct overview of your business. Incorporate your statement of purpose, a concise portrayal of your items or services, and your essential objectives. This part ought to convey what your business does and why it makes a difference.

Then, detail your business description. Explain your hobby's change into a business, the specialty you serve, and what makes your contributions novel. For instance, assuming that your hobby is creating eco-accommodating candles, feature how your reasonable strategy separates you from the market.

The market analysis segment exhibits how you might interpret the business and target audience. Remember to research market patterns, customer socioeconomics, and contenders. Show how your business fills a hole on the lookout or meets a neglected need.

The task plan frames how your business will work every day. Examine your production cycle, supply chain, and conveyance strategies. If you're an independent business person, make sense of how you oversee undertakings productively; assuming you intend to scale, detail how you'll construct a group or rethink liabilities.

At long last, incorporate a financial arrangement. Outline your pricing procedure, projected income, and anticipated costs. While precise numbers may not be accessible, evaluations can assist you with defining reasonable objectives and tracking your financial health after some time.

## Financial Projections and Budgeting Fundamentals

Financial projections are a basic part of your strategy, offering knowledge of the feasibility of your business. Begin by pricing your income in light of market interest, evaluating, and sales channels. For example, assuming you hope to sell 100 high-quality cleansers month to month at $15 each, your projected monthly income would be $1,500.

Then, ascertain your expected costs. These incorporate both fixed costs (e.g., hardware, site facilitating, or licensing charges) and variable expenses (e.g., materials, bundling, and delivery). Deduct these costs from your income to estimate your overall revenues.

Making a budget assists you with managing resources successfully and keeping away from superfluous spending. Partition your budget into classifications like creation, promotion, and functional expenses. Distribute resources to every category in light of your business needs. For instance, if you're simply beginning, you could allot more resources to advertising to construct brand awareness.

Use tools like calculation sheets or budgeting applications to follow costs and monitor income. Regularly survey your funds to guarantee you're remaining focused and change your budget as needed.

## Setting Short-term and Long-term Goals

Goals are the groundwork of a fruitful marketable strategy. They give an internal direction and a system for pricing progress. Partition your targets into momentary objectives (feasible in something like a half year to a year) and long-term objectives (spanning several years).

Short-term goals could incorporate launching your site, getting your first 50 customers, or accomplishing a particular income success. These goals ought to be significant and time-bound. For instance, rather than defining a dubious objective like "increase sales," go for the gold "in income in six months or less."

Turning Your Hobby into a 6-Figure

Long-term goals focus on a more extensive vision for your business. These could incorporate venturing into new business sectors, broadening your product offering, or procuring a six-figure income every year. Long-term goals ought to line up with your main goal and reflect where you see your business in the future.

To guarantee a positive outcome, take on the SMART goals structure — goals that are Specific, Quantifiable, Reachable, Significant, and Time-bound. For instance, if you intend to extend your product offering, determine the number of new items, set a realistic timetable, and framework moves toward accomplishing this goal.

Regularly return to your goals to evaluate progress and adapt. Praising success along the way can keep you propelled and give you a feeling of success.

A winning market plan is your directing light, assisting you with exploring difficulties, immediately jumping all over chances, and remaining fixed on your vision. By improving on the arranging system, establishing your financial projections truly, and setting clear targets, you will create a strong starting point for manageable development and long-term success.

## Part 3: Attracting and Growing Your Customer Base

# CHAPTER 7: MARKETING YOUR HOBBY BUSINESS EFFECTIVELY

**Leveraging Social Media and Digital Marketing**

In the present digital age, social media platforms are useful resources for marketing your hobby business. They offer chances to interface with your audience, showcase your items, and build a conspicuous brand — all without requiring a heavy marketing financial plan.

Begin by recognizing the platforms where your target audience is generally active. For instance, visually determined platforms like Instagram or Pinterest are great for businesses that sell high-quality or creative items. If your hobby business takes special care of experts, LinkedIn may be a superior decision.

Making a steady satisfying strategy is key to fruitful social media promotion. Share great pictures or recordings of your items, give in-the-background looks into your cycle, and propose significant hints connected with your specialty. For example, on the off chance that you maintain a baking business, you could share short instructional exercises on icing strategies or recipes including your items.

Integrate storytelling to humanize your brand. Share your journey of transforming a passion into a business and interface genuinely with your audience. Utilize appealing hashtags to increment discoverability and connect effectively with your adherents by answering remarks, direct messages, and reviews.

Advanced marketing goes past social media. Consider beginning a blog or email pamphlet to furnish inside and out happiness that reverberates with your audience. Expound on themes that line up with your business, for example, patterns in your specialty or instructional exercises exhibiting your mastery. Match these endeavors with site design improvement (Search engine optimization) to expand visibility and direct people to your site.

Paid advertising can likewise intensify your range. Platforms like Facebook and Google Advertisements offer designated promoting choices, licensing you to arrive at potential customers in view of socio economics, interests, and ways of behaving. Begin little, test different promotion designs, and refine your procedure in light of the performance analysis.

**Building an Engaged Audience**
An engaged audience is the soul of your hobby business. The way to build such an audience of people lies in cultivating real connections and offering steady benefits.

Start by understanding your audience's preferences, difficulties, and desires. Lead reviews, polls, or casual feedback to accumulate bits of knowledge. Utilize this data to make content that impacts them. For instance, if your audience values eco-awareness, feature the supportable practices behind your items.

Commitment flourishes with credibility. Share engaging stories about your enterprising journey, showcase customer tributes, or feature how your items affect your customers' lives. Genuineness assembles trust, making your audience bound to help and backer for your business.

Boost commitment through intuitive drives. Have challenges, giveaways, or difficulties that urge your audience to take an interest. For example, on the off chance that you sell hand-tailored jewelry, a photograph challenge demanding that customers share how they style your pieces could ignite fervor and widen your range.

Leverage user-generated content (UGC) to reinforce your local area. Reposting customer photographs, reviews, or stories approves your brand as well as develops connections with your audience. Continuously look for consent and credit the first creators to keep up with generosity.

Consistency is essential in audience building. Post regularly through social media, send pamphlets on an anticipated timetable, and answer speedily to demand or remarks. An anticipated musicality assists your audience with having an associated and informed outlook on your brand.

Turning Your Hobby into a 6-Figure

**Content Creation Tips for the Most Extreme Effect**
Creating valuable content is all about delivering the right message to the right audience effectively. To produce meaningful content, start by aligning your information with your brand's core values and mission. Your content should reflect your passion for your craft and demonstrate the unique value your business offers.

Visual content is particularly effective for hobby businesses. Invest in quality photography or video production to effectively showcase your products or services. Even a basic smartphone camera, combined with good lighting and composition, can produce professional-looking visuals. Broaden your substance configurations to keep your audience locked in. Combine item exhibits with instructional exercises, tributes, in background recordings, and live round-table discussions. Try different things with various styles to see what reverberates most with your audience.

Storytelling is a distinct advantage. Share the story behind your brand, feature customer encounters, or show how your items take care of normal issues. Stories are paramount and assist your audience with interfacing sincerely with your brand.

Leverage analytics to upgrade your content procedure. Most social media platforms and site tools give information on commitment, reach, and audience socioeconomics. Utilize these bits of knowledge to refine your content, focusing on what performs well and changing or ending what doesn't.

Marketing your hobby business really is about more than promoting items — it's tied in with making significant connections with your audience and building a local area around your brand. By utilizing digital tools, connecting genuinely with your audience, and conveying significant content, you can lay out serious areas of strength that drive long-term success.

# CHAPTER 8: SELLING STRATEGIES FOR SUCCESS

**Exploring Sales Channels (Online, in-Person, Wholesale)**
Distinguishing the right sales channels is a basic move toward scaling your hobby business. Each channel offers unique advantages and difficulties, so understanding their elements assists you with augmenting productivity while keeping up with functional proficiency.

Online sales channels have turned into a foundation for present day businesses. Platforms like Etsy, Amazon Hand tailored, and Shopify are great for specialists progressing into business. They permit you to exhibit your items to a worldwide audience, frequently with insignificant startup costs. Improve your online-based customer-facing facade by including great pictures, clear item descriptions, and pricing information. Try not to disregard customer reviews, as they build trust and drive changes.

Social media platforms likewise double as strong sales channels. Highlights like Instagram Shopping and Facebook Commercial focus make it simple for customers to find and buy your items. Utilize these tools decisively by incorporating shoppable posts and coordinating traffic on your site or store.

For the people who favor individual connections, in-person sales channels like local specialty fairs, ranchers' business sectors, and spring-up shops offer significant opportunities. These scenes let you build connections with customers, get immediate feedback, and lay out a presence locally. Setting up an enticing showcase stall, giving examples, and connecting energetically with guests are fundamental for outcomes in these spaces.

Wholesale is another avenue for development, especially assuming you produce things in mass. Collaborating with retailers can extend your scope and give you a consistent income stream. Move toward likely collaborates with an expert pitch that incorporates pricing, demand essentials, and conveyance courses of events. Guarantee your items line up with their audience and store feel to expand your possibilities of cooperation.

A broadened approach — combining on the online, face to face, and wholesale channels — can assist with moderating dangers and expand income. Survey your resources, objectives, and customer preferences to decide the best blend for your business.

**Building Connections with Customers**

Strong customer connections are the groundwork for long-term success. At the point when customers feel valued, they are bound to become recurrent purchasers and promoters for your business.

Begin by giving remarkable customer care. Answer speedily to demand, resolve issues expertly, and finish guarantees. These little motions have enduring effects and construct trust.

Engage with your audience regularly to cultivate connection. Social media platforms, email bulletins, and devotion programs are amazing instruments for remaining top-of-mind. Share updates about your business, offer select discounts, or just thank your customers for their help.

Personalization upgrades connections. Use customer names in messages, tailor item proposals in light of past buys, and celebrate successes like birthday celebrations or commemorations with unique offers. These signals show that you care about your customers past the exchange.

Encourage feedback and follow up on it. Demand reviews or ideas to work on your contributions, and openly thank customers who carve out opportunities to give input. At the point when customers see that their perspectives matter, they foster a more grounded liking for your brand.

At long last, create a sense of community around your business. Have occasions, whether on online or face-to-face, where customers can interface with you and one another. For instance, on the off chance that your hobby includes making, sort out studios where customers can learn new methods while utilizing your items. Building connections is about more than selling — about making significant connections cultivated unwaveringly.

## Closing Deals and Generating Repeat Business

Bringing a deal to a close isn't the finish of the customer venture; it's the start of a relationship. To close deals effectively, you want to figure out your customers' requirements and communicate the value of your items.

While associating with likely purchasers, focus on tending to their trouble spots or goals. For instance, assuming your hobby business includes making custom organizers, underscore how your item can assist customers with remaining coordinated and useful. Offer clear, succinct clarifications of your items' advantages, and expect normal objections by getting ready insightful reactions.

Creating urgency can likewise propel customers to make a buy. Restricted time offers, selective discounts, or occasional promotions are viable procedures for driving activity. Guarantee your information is certified and lined up with your brand values to keep up with the credibility.

After completing the initial transaction, focus on converting one-time buyers into repeat customers. Follow up with a thank-you email or message, and consider including a discount code for their next purchase. Maintaining consistent communication, such as personalized recommendations or updates about new products, helps keep your business at the forefront of their minds.

Loyalty programs are one more incredible asset for producing repeat business. Offer compensations for incessant buys, references, or social media shares. These impetuses energize repeat exchanges as well as extend customer reliability.

At long last, monitor your customer retention measurements to recognize areas for development. Measurements, like repeat buy rate or customer lifetime value, give experiences into your business' exhibition and feature amazing chances to fortify your selling strategies.

Selling is a craftsmanship that extends beyond the exchange. By investigating different sales channels, building significant connections, and focusing on customer retention, you can make a manageable business that flourishes with dedication and trust. A customer driven approach guarantees that your hobby business proceeds to develop and prosper in the competitive marketplace.

# CHAPTER 9: THE POWER OF NETWORKING AND COLLABORATION

**Finding Mentors and Joining Communities**

Networking is a basic expertise for entrepreneurs hoping to raise their hobby business. Encircling yourself with experienced guides and similar people gives significant bits of knowledge, backing, and amazing opportunities.

Finding a mentor is a unique advantage. Mentors bring insight and pragmatic guidance from their innovative journeys. Look for people who have insight into your industry or who have effectively scaled businesses from scratch. Begin by investigating local business connections, going to industry occasions, or joining on online platforms like LinkedIn. While moving toward a possible tutor, being specific about your objectives and how you accept their direction could help. Recognize their time by being ready with focused questions and clear targets.

Joining a group of specialists or business visionaries offers an alternate but similarly significant viewpoint. Online communities, for example, Facebook groups, Reddit forums, or industry-specific platforms are unique spots to interface with individuals who share your interests. Local meetups or cooperating spaces additionally give chances to trade thoughts, share difficulties, and assemble significant connections.

Networks offer a help framework where individuals praise each other's successes, offer valuable input, and team up on projects. Encircling yourself with driven and steady people cultivates responsibility and inspiration. Through mentorship and active local area contribution, you get sufficiently access to an abundance of information, best practices, and resources that can speed up your development.

**Partnerships with Complementary Businesses**

Coordinated effort with corresponding businesses is an essential method for developing your audience and extending your range. An integral business offers items or services that line up with yours but don't straightforwardly contend. These businesses set out commonly useful opportunities to cross-advance and increase customer commitment.

For instance, in the event that your hobby business includes high quality candles, collaborating with a local craftsman who makes earthenware for candle holders can upgrade the allure of your items. Together, you could make packaged contributions or co-have occasions to draw in new customers.

While looking for partnerships, focus around businesses that share your qualities and target audience. Connect with an unmistakable proposition enumerating how the joint effort will help the two players. Be specific about your objectives, whether it's rising sales, growing your customer base, or reinforcing your brand's standing.

Building trust is fundamental in partnerships. Keep up with open communication, obviously define roles and obligations, and lay out terms that guarantee shared accomplishment. A strong organization supports your business as well as encourages generosity and long-term proficient connections.

## Scaling Through Strategic Collaborations efforts

Vital collaborations efforts go past one-off partnerships; they include purposeful endeavors to line up with people or businesses that intensify your business' effect. These joint efforts can incorporate influencers, bigger businesses, or philanthropic connections, contingent upon your objectives and vision.

Working with influencers is a cutting edge method for extending your audience. Micro-influencers, specifically, frequently have emotionally connected with devotees who trust their suggestions. Joining forces with them to showcase your items acquaints your brand with new customers. Guarantee that the influencers you pick line up with your brand values and talk really to their audience.

Turning Your Hobby into a 6-Figure

Teaming up with bigger businesses can likewise open ways to huge opportunities. For instance, licensing your designs to a notable retailer can bring financial advantages and expanded visibility. Move toward these joint efforts expertly, introducing your business' remarkable value and showing how the connection would be valuable together.

Philanthropic collaboration efforts are another strong procedure. Cooperating with magnanimous businesses permits you to interface with customers on a more emotional level by adjusting your brand to a significant reason. For example, giving a part of sales to natural drives if your hobby business focuses on eco-accommodating items can reverberate unequivocally with socially cognizant customers.

Vital collaboration efforts require cautious preparation and execution. Set clear targets, make itemized arrangements, and measure the effect of these businesses. The right collaboration efforts can drive your hobby business into new business sectors and cement your situation as a trusted and creative brand.

Networking and collaboration efforts are not simply tools for developing your business — they're investments in your future. By associating with mentors, engaging with communities, and forming vital businesses, you lay the foundation for long-term success. Collaboration effort encourages imagination, grows your reach, and supports the strength of your brand, guaranteeing that your hobby business flourishes in the present competitive marketplace.

# Part 4: Scaling and Sustaining Growth

# CHAPTER 10: AUTOMATING AND STREAMLINING OPERATIONS

**Investing in Tools and Software**

As your hobby business develops, physically taking care of every errand becomes tedious and limits your capability to scale. Automation tools and programming smooth out activities, save time and guarantee consistency. Technology is your partner in working on processes, from managing stock to drawing in with customers.

Begin by distinguishing the dull tasks in your work process. Normal areas to automate incorporate accounting, email marketing, customer relationship management (CRM), and booking. For instance, bookkeeping programming like QuickBooks or FreshBooks works on following costs and producing solicitations. Email marketing platforms like Mailchimp or Steady Contact can automate missions and sustain customer connections.

Online businesses can profit from platforms like Shopify or WooCommerce, which coordinate installment handling, stock service, and investigation into one framework. Social media management instruments like Cradle or Hootsuite permit you to plan posts across various platforms, guaranteeing steady commitment with your audience.

While choosing tools, focus on those that incorporate consistently with your current frameworks. Pick versatile arrangements that can adjust to your business' development. While automation requires an underlying venture, the long-term reserve funds in time and effort outweigh the expenses, licensing you to focus in on essential areas of your business.

**Delegating and Outsourcing Tasks**

No effective business person builds a flourishing business alone. Delegating and re-appropriating tasks is fundamental to keeping up with efficiency and staying balanced. Delegation permits you to focus in on high-influence exercises while entrusting normal or particular undertakings to other people.

Begin by recognizing tasks that consume your time or fall outside your ability. Authoritative obligations, social media, management, visual description, and customer service are normal areas for reevaluating. Platforms like Fiverr, Upwork, and Toptal connect you with gifted experts around the world, offering adaptable and practical arrangements.

While recruiting, obviously define the extent of work, courses of events, and assumptions. Direct meetings or survey portfolios to guarantee you're working with the right fit. Communication is of the utmost importance for effective delegation — lay out standard registrations to monitor progress and address any issues.

For in-house tasks, think about building a little group to deal with tasks. Whether it's a part time partner to oversee orders or a committed marketing master, having a strong group guarantees smoother tasks. Engage your group by giving clear directions, preparing, and admittance to important instruments. Delegation isn't just about offloading tasks; it is about making an emotionally supportive network move your business forward.

**Building a Group for Development**
As your hobby business changes into an undeniable enterprise, building a group becomes fundamental for supported development. A strong group increases effectiveness as well as brings different viewpoints and abilities that improve your business.

Define the roles your business needs founded on its ongoing difficulties and future objectives. For example, on the off chance that if managing demand has become overpowering, a satisfaction expert may be your most memorable recruit. If extending your brand presence is fundamentally important, consider employing a promoting planner or social media director.

Focus around making a positive organizational culture that mirrors your qualities. Indeed, even in private companies, cultivating a climate of coordinated effort and regard draws in and holds top ability. Be straightforward about your vision and guarantee your colleagues understand how their roles add to the master plan.

Leverage technology to deal with your group. Tools like Asana, Trello, or Slack smoothly streamline communication and task management, guaranteeing everybody stays adjusted. Consistently assess group performance, celebrate success, and give opportunities for development and advancement.

Recruiting is an investment, so move toward it decisively. The right group speeds up your progress, licensing you to focus on development and scaling. Building a group is about more than filling positions — about making a durable unit that shares your vision and cooperates to accomplish it.

Automating activities, delegating tasks, and building a group are the foundations of scaling your hobby business productively. By coordinating the right instruments, reevaluating intelligently, and collecting a devoted group, you make a vigorous starting point for development. These strategies permit you to move from managing everyday tasks to directing your business toward long-term success, guaranteeing that your passion-driven enterprise keeps on flourishing.

# CHAPTER 11: DIVERSIFYING YOUR INCOME STREAMS

**Expanding Product/Service Offerings**

Diversifying your revenue streams starts with growing the scope of items or services your business offers. A more extensive portfolio draws in new customers as well as furnishes existing ones with additional ways of connecting with your brand, expanding their lifetime value.

To begin, survey your focus contributions and distinguish reciprocal items or services. For instance, assuming that your hobby includes making high-quality adornments, you could add customization choices, present occasional collections, or sell care packs for jewelry upkeep. Service-based businesses, similar to photography, can broaden by offering studios, customized photograph collections, or digital altering services.

Pay attention to your customers — they are an important source of motivation. Studies, reviews, and direct feedback can uncover neglected needs or wants that your business can satisfy. Be key while extending your contributions to guarantee they line up with your brand's personality and values.

Pilot new items or services on a limited scale before a full launch. This permits you to measure interest, accumulate feedback, and make fundamental changes without a huge gamble. An iterative strategy guarantees your broadening endeavors meet customer assumptions and improve your general brand value.

**Setting out Passive Revenue Opportunities**

Passive income empowers your business to economically procure income with negligible continuous effort, making them a useful asset for scaling. These opportunities frequently include making resources that produce pay over the long run.

One well-known avenue is digital items. digital books, online courses, layouts, or configuration records can be made once and sold over and again. For example, a painter could sell downloadable prints of their work, while a weaving lover could offer digital designs. Platforms like Gumroad, Etsy, or your site make it simple to sell digital products straightforwardly to customers.

Another choice is subscription-based services. A monthly subscription box tailored to your specialty can give customers organized things while guaranteeing steady income. On the other hand, admittance to elite content, like instructional exercises or background experiences, can be monetized through platforms like Patreon.

Affiliate marketing is another successful strategy. Partner with brands or businesses that align with your values and earn commissions by promoting their products. Ensure your recommendations are authentic and relevant to maintain the trust of your audience.

Finally, consider allowing your work to be licensed. If your hobby involves creating unique designs or proprietary technology, licensing agreements can provide a steady stream of royalties without requiring you to produce or sell the products yourself. Passive income sources not only stabilize your earnings but also free up resources for other development-focused activities.

**Licensing and Affiliate Marketing**
Licensing permits, you to use the compass and resources of laid-out brands while holding command over your protected technology. This technique includes conceding different businesses the option to deliver, circulate, or sell items highlighting your designs or manifestations.

To explore licensing opportunities, recognize businesses or brands that line up with your taste or market. For instance, a craftsman could permit their designs to writing material makers, or a cook could permit their recipes to a food brand. Negotiate arrangements cautiously to guarantee you get fair remuneration while safeguarding your innovative freedoms. Licensing agreements can give reliable income insignificant info, making them an appealing choice for scaling your business.

Affiliate marketing is another value while revenue source. By cooperating with brands and advancing their items through your foundation, you can acquire commissions for every deal created through your reference. For example, a photographic artist could suggest camera hardware, while a wellness devotee could advance exercise gear.

Pick affiliate partnerships decisively to keep up with validity. Just support items that reverberate with your brand and proposition of authentic value to your audience. The straightforward revelation of member connections assembles a trust and urges your audience to help with your recommendations.

Platforms like Amazon Partners or ShareASale make it simple to track down affiliate opportunities across different enterprises. By integrating member joins into your content — for example, blog posts, social media, or YouTube videos — you can generate recurring, automated revenue while enhancing your audience's experience.

**The Advantages of Income Diversification**

Diversifying your revenue streams is more than a development system; it's a way to future-proof your business. Depending exclusively on one item, service, or income source leaves you helpless against market fluctuations or changing customer preferences. A broadened pay portfolio gives financial soundness and flexibility, guaranteeing your business flourishes even in challenging times.

Besides, offering various items or services increases customer devotion. At the point when customers track down different ways of drawing in with your brand, they are bound to return and prescribe your business to other people. This reinforces your standing and builds a local area around your contributions.

Diversification likewise opens new opportunities for creativity and development. By investigating different income streams, you challenge yourself to figure past your essential contribution, pushing the limits of what your business can accomplish.

Taking everything into account, pay broadening is fundamental for long-term success. Whether through extending your contributions, setting out automated revenue opportunities, or utilizing licensing and affiliate marketing, these techniques engage your business to develop reasonably while lessening risk. By embracing diversification, you make a flourishing, versatile venture equipped for enduring any challenge.

## CHAPTER 12: OVERCOMING CHALLENGES IN SCALING

**Navigating Financial Hurdles**

Scaling a business frequently requires critical financial investment, and exploring these obstacles is a vital part of supportable development. Normal difficulties incorporate income imperatives, surprising costs, and the requirement for financing to help development.

To address income issues, consider carrying out systems that balance out pay and limit costs. Offering subscription models, pre-sales, or installment designs can make a consistent income stream. Monitor your financials consistently to distinguish examples and settle on informed conclusions about spending and investment. Utilizing bookkeeping programming or recruiting a financial counsel can smooth out this cycle and give significant experience.

To handle unforeseen costs, it's important to set aside a financial cushion or backup fund. Save a portion of your profits each month to create a safety net for unexpected expenses. This proactive approach reduces stress and ensures that your business can navigate challenges without hindering its growth.

Getting financing for scaling can include exploring different choices, for example, business credits, awards, or investors. Research awards and projects that cater specifically to private businesses in your specialty. On the other hand, audience funding platforms like Kickstarter or Indiegogo can give subsidies while at the same time assembling customer interest and loyalty. While looking for investors, focus on the people who line up with your business values and bring something other than capital — like expertise or industry connections.

**Adjusting to Market Changes**

The business scene is continually developing, and adjusting to showcase changes is fundamental for long-term success. Whether driven by financial movements, mechanical advancements, or changing customer preferences, the capacity to turn guarantees your business stays important and competitive.

Remain informed by directing ordinary statistical surveying. Monitor patterns in your industry, track rivals' strategies, and pay attention to customer feedback to expect changes. Instruments like Google Patterns, social media analytics, and customer overviews can give important information on arising demand and preferences.

Adaptability is basic while adjusting to change. For instance, on the off chance that your hobby business is vigorously dependent on in-person sales and market patterns demonstrate a shift toward internet business, think about putting resources into an online-based store or working on your current digital presence. Essentially, diversifying in items or services can assist your business with taking care of changing customer needs and diminishing reliance on a solitary income source.

Embrace innovation to remain on top of things. This could include taking on new advances, investigating supportable practices, or presenting inventive advertising strategies. Innovation assists you with adjusting as well as positioning your business as a groundbreaking pioneer in your specialty.

**Keeping up with Balance between fun and serious activities**
As your business develops, keeping up with a balance between fun and serious activities turns out to be progressively difficult but fundamental for supporting both individual prosperity and expert success. Overstretching yourself can prompt burnout, diminished efficiency, and stressed connections, sabotaging your endeavors to successfully scale.

Focus on taking care of oneself by defining clear limits between work and individual life. Assign specific hours for business undertakings and stick to them, allowing yourself to re-energize and focus on different parts of life. Discuss these limits with your group and customers to lay out expectations and safeguard your own time.

Delegate and outsource tasks to decrease your responsibility and let loose passion for vital independent direction. Enlist representatives, specialists, or menial helpers for obligations that don't need your immediate contribution. This mitigates pressure as well as permits you to focus on areas where you add the most value.

Putting resources into instruments and technology that smooth out tasks can likewise assist with keeping up with balance. Automation programming, project management tools, and customer relationship management (CRM) systems work on monotonous tasks and further develop effectiveness, giving you additional opportunities for individual and expert development.

Develop an encouraging group of people of family, friends, and coaches who figure out your difficulties and can give direction and consolation. Imparting encounters with different business visionaries can offer important experiences and advise you that you are in good company to explore the intricacies of scaling a business.

**Overcoming Common Growth Difficulties**
Scaling a business accompanies its own set of difficulties, including managing expanded demand, keeping up with quality, and protecting the quintessence of your brand. Proactively resolving these issues is basic to supporting development without compromising consumer loyalty or brand honesty.

Managing expanded demand requires cautious preparation and asset distribution. Expect development by guaranteeing your creation processes, stock levels, and staffing can meet higher volumes. Normalize work processes and layout alternate courses of action to forestall bottlenecks or postponements.

Keeping up with quality is fundamental as your business scales. Guarantee consistency by archiving standard operating procedures (SOPs) and preparing your group to maintain these guidelines. Consistently demand customer feedback to recognize areas for development and show your obligation to greatness.

Saving your brand's identity during development is similarly significant. Remain consistent with your basic beliefs and mission, guaranteeing that development endeavors line up with your unique vision. Consistency in informing, visuals, and customer communications supports your brand's genuineness and encourages faithfulness.

Scaling may likewise include beating individual questions or an inability to acknowledge success. Encircle yourself with a strong emotionally supportive network and help yourself to remember the successes you've accomplished up to this point. Trust in your vision and capacities will enable you to deal with challenges directly and lead your business higher than ever.

**The Way to Strong Development**
Overcoming challenges in scaling a business requires careful preparation, adaptability, and persistence. By addressing financial obstacles, staying attuned to market changes, balancing enjoyable and serious activities, and proactively managing common growth challenges, you can build a business that not only survives but thrives.

Each challenge presents an opportunity to learn, grow, and strengthen your foundation. With the right mindset and strategies, you can turn obstacles into stepping stones, ensuring your business remains robust and poised for long-term success.

## Part 5: Thriving as a 6-Figure Business Owner

# CHAPTER 13: MASTERING YOUR ENTREPRENEURIAL MINDSET

**Staying Motivated During Highs and Lows**

Entrepreneurship is a journey filled with peaks and valleys, and staying inspired through these fluctuations is essential for long-term success. While the highs can boost your motivation, the lows may challenge your resilience. Developing strategies to maintain inspiration ensures that you stay on track, regardless of external circumstances.

Start by reconnecting with your "why." Reflect on the reasons you began your entrepreneurial journey and the goals you aim to achieve. This sense of purpose serves as a powerful source of motivation during challenging times. Write down your mission statement and revisit it regularly to remind yourself of your vision.

Celebrate your successes, no matter how small. Acknowledging progress builds momentum and reinforces your confidence in your abilities. Whether it's achieving a revenue milestone or receiving positive feedback from customers, take the time to appreciate your accomplishments and use them as motivation to keep moving forward.

During difficult periods, seek inspiration from the stories of other successful entrepreneurs who have overcome setbacks. Their journeys can offer valuable insights and remind you that challenges are a natural part of the process. Surround yourself with supportive people who encourage you to persevere and maintain a positive outlook.

Finally, establish a routine that balances productivity and self-care. Incorporate activities that refresh and inspire you, such as exercise, meditation, or hobbies unrelated to your business. Maintaining your physical and mental well-being lays the foundation for sustained motivation and success.

## Learning from Failures and Mistakes

Failure is an unavoidable piece of business; however, it can likewise be quite possible for the best instructor. Each difficulty gives an amazing chance to learn, adjust, and develop. Moving your point of view to see failure as a stepping stone, as opposed to a barrier, is critical to dominating your entrepreneurial mindset.

Dissect failures unbiasedly by asking yourself what turned out badly and for what valid reason. Search for examples or choices that might have added to the result and recognize specific areas for development. This course of reflection transforms mistakes into significant examples.

Embrace a development mindset by survey moves as any opportunities to foster new abilities or refine existing ones. For example, if a promoting effort doesn't yield the ideal outcomes, use it as an opportunity to develop how you might interpret your audience and investigate alternative systems.

Keep away from the trap of self-fault. All things being equal, focus on responsibility and critical thinking. Assume a sense of ownership with your activities while perceiving outside factors that might have impacted the circumstance. This reasonable strategy permits you to push ahead with clearness and certainty.

Share your encounters with others, whether through mentorship, networking, or public talking. By straightforwardly examining your failures, you standardize the growing experience and motivate others to continue through their difficulties.

## Developing Strength for Long-term Success

Resilience is the foundation of a pioneering mindset, empowering you to weather conditions difficulties and arise more grounded. Building resilience requires a mix of mental, emotional, and functional systems that set you up to adjust and flourish notwithstanding difficulty.

Begin by creating the capacity to appreciate individuals on an emotional level, which includes perceiving and dealing with your feelings successfully. Practice care to remain present and grounded, particularly during high-pressure circumstances. This mindfulness assists you with moving toward difficulties with a quiet and focused mindset.

Build an emotionally supportive network of coaches, peers, friends, and family who can give direction, consolation, and productive feedback. Having an organization to rest on during difficult times builds up your versatility and reminds you that you are in good company in your journey.

Versatility is one more key part of resilience. Embrace change as a characteristic piece of business and view it as a valuable chance to innovate. By remaining open to new thoughts and approaches, you position yourself to answer proactively to moving conditions.

Resilience likewise comes from keeping a good overall balance between work and individual life. Regularly detach from business-related stressors to re-energize your passion and perspective. This balance guarantees you remain genuinely and intellectually prepared to deal with the demands of entrepreneurship.

**Embracing the Enterprising Journey**

Dominating your innovative mindset is certainly not a one-time accomplishment but a continuous cycle. It requires constant self-reflection, learning, and development. By remaining persuaded during ups and downs, gaining from failures, and developing resilience, you develop the psychological and emotional fortitude expected to explore the intricacies of business proprietorship.

Recall that success is as much about the journey as what it's value about the objective. Embrace the lessons, connections, and encounters that accompany being a business person. By encouraging a mindset established in passion, versatility, and assurance, you set yourself up not exclusively to accomplish your objectives but additionally to partake during the time spent building something significant and effective.

# Conclusion

Turning your hobby into a 6-figure business is a journey of passion, reason, and tirelessness. This book has furnished you with the fundamental tools to distinguish a beneficial hobby, make a convincing business vision, lay out areas of strength for a, and construct feasible development. Key focal points incorporate understanding your market, making a remarkable brand, and dominating procedures for evaluating, marketing, and scaling tasks.

Success lies in action. Start by surveying your hobby's true capacity and putting forth sensible objectives. Embrace the method involved with learning and adjusting, utilizing each test as a chance to develop. Assemble significant connections, team up in a calculated manner, and remain focused on conveying value to your customers.

Above all, recollect that entrepreneurship is about more than financial success. It's tied in with making every moment count, making influence, and accomplishing satisfaction based on your conditions. Remain strong, continue to refine your abilities, and sustain a mindset that embraces change and development.

Your 6-figure business is reachable. With the means and procedures framed in this book, you have all that you want to transform your passion into a flourishing venture. Take the jump, trust the cycle, and watch your vision become completely awake. The journey starts today.

www.ingramcontent.com/pod-product-compliance
Lightning Source LLC
Chambersburg PA
CBHW070948220526
45471CB00007B/2935